Crafts to Make in the Spring

CRAFTS
FOR ALL
SEASONS

Crafts
to make
in the
Spring

KATHY ROSS

Illustrated by Vicky Enright

The Millbrook Press   Brookfield, Connecticut

For my sister, Badar — K.R.

For my dad, Victor S. Kraft,
with love and thanks for all. —V.E.

Library of Congress Cataloging-in-Publication Data
Ross, Kathy (Katharine Reynolds), 1948–
Crafts to make in the spring Kathy Ross ; illustrated by Vicky Enright.
p.   cm. — (Crafts for all seasons)
Summary: Presents twenty-nine easy-to-make craft projects with springtime
themes, including cotton swab pussy willows, a robin redbreast door hanging,
and an Easter bunny egg holder.
ISBN 0-7613-0316-2 (lib. bdg.). — ISBN 0-7613-0333-2 (pbk.)
1. Handicraft—Juvenile literature. 2. Spring—Juvenile literature. [1. Handicraft.
2. Spring.] I. Enright, Vicky, ill. II. Title. III. Series: Ross, Kathy (Katharine
Reynolds), 1948– Crafts for all seasons.
TT160.R71425   1998
745.5—dc2l   97-24644
CIP   AC

Published by The Millbrook Press, Inc.
2 Old New Milford Road
Brookfield, Connecticut 06804

Contents

For many, pussy willows are one of the first signs of spring.

Cotton Swab Pussy Willows

Here is what you need:

cotton swabs (about 30)

two 12-inch (30-cm) brown pipe cleaners

pencil

one sheet of blue construction paper

stapler

piece of wallpaper

yarn

gray poster paint

scissors

white glue

Styrofoam tray for drying

Here is what you do:

1 Dip both ends of the cotton swabs in the gray paint. Put the swabs on the Styrofoam tray to dry.

2 Draw a vase on the back of the wallpaper. Make it a little less than half as tall as the piece of construction paper. Cut the vase out.

3 Cut each pipe cleaner in two so that one piece is slightly longer than the other piece.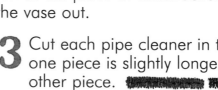

4 Glue the wallpaper vase onto the construction paper, putting the four pieces of pipe cleaner into the vase to look like stems.

5 Cut the gray ends off of each of the cotton swabs. For the pussy-willow buds, glue the fuzzy gray swab ends along the sides of each of the pipe-cleaner stems.

6 Cut a 24 inch (61-cm) piece of yarn. Fold the top inch (2.5 cm) of the picture back. Put the middle part of the yarn under the fold and staple the fold to hold it in place. Tie the two ends of the yarn together to make a hanger.

Meow!

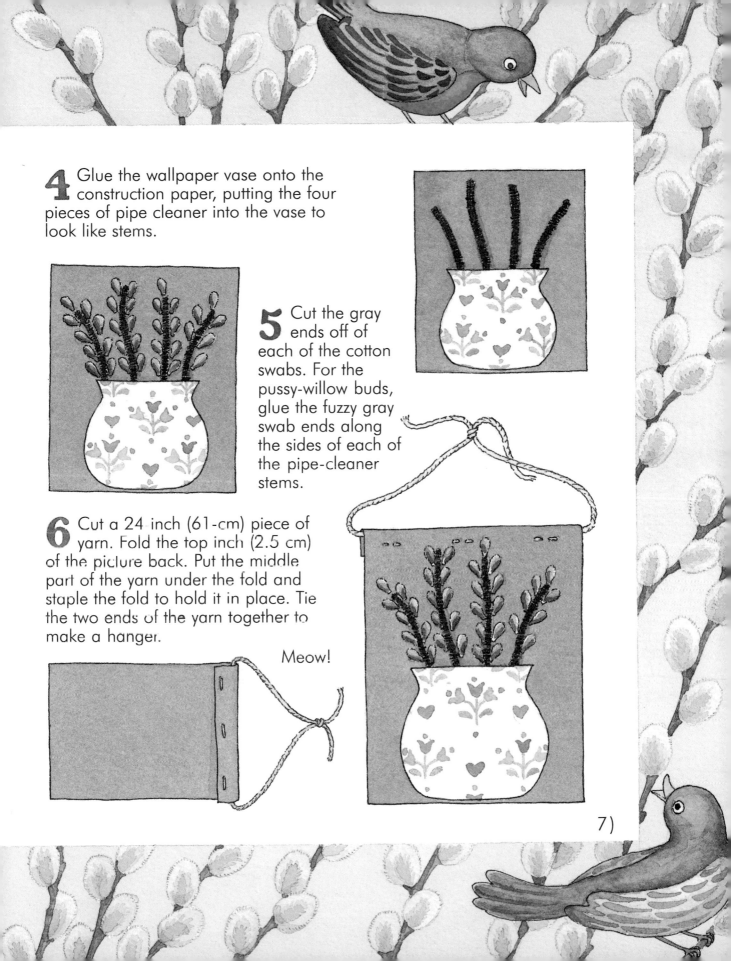

**Spotting a robin is a sure sign
of the coming of spring.**

Robin Redbreast Door Hanging

Here is what you need:

 four 9-inch (23-cm)
paper plates

 two 6-inch (15-cm) paper plates

 one 6½-inch (17-cm) paper bowl

 white glue

stapler

 scissors

 red and brown poster paint
and a paintbrush

 one 12-inch (30-cm)
brown pipe cleaner

white, black, and
orange paper

newspaper
to work on

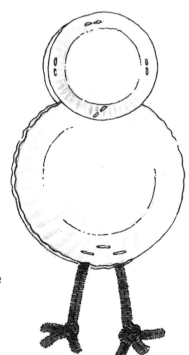

Here is what you do:

1 Fold the pipe cleaner in half. Cut a 1-inch (2.5-cm) piece off each end. To make a foot, bend the end of the pipe cleaner out and wrap the 1-inch piece around the foot to make toes. Repeat for the other foot. Staple two of the larger plates together with the bent pipe cleaner between them so that the legs hang down from the plate body.

2 Staple the two smaller plates together on one side. Slide the edge of one plate over the top front of the body and the other plate over the back. Staple the plates in place to make the head of the bird.

(8

FLORIDA
TEXAS

3 Fold the two remaining plates in half. Staple one over each side of the body to form the wings.

4 Paint the entire bird brown. Paint the bottom of the bowl red.

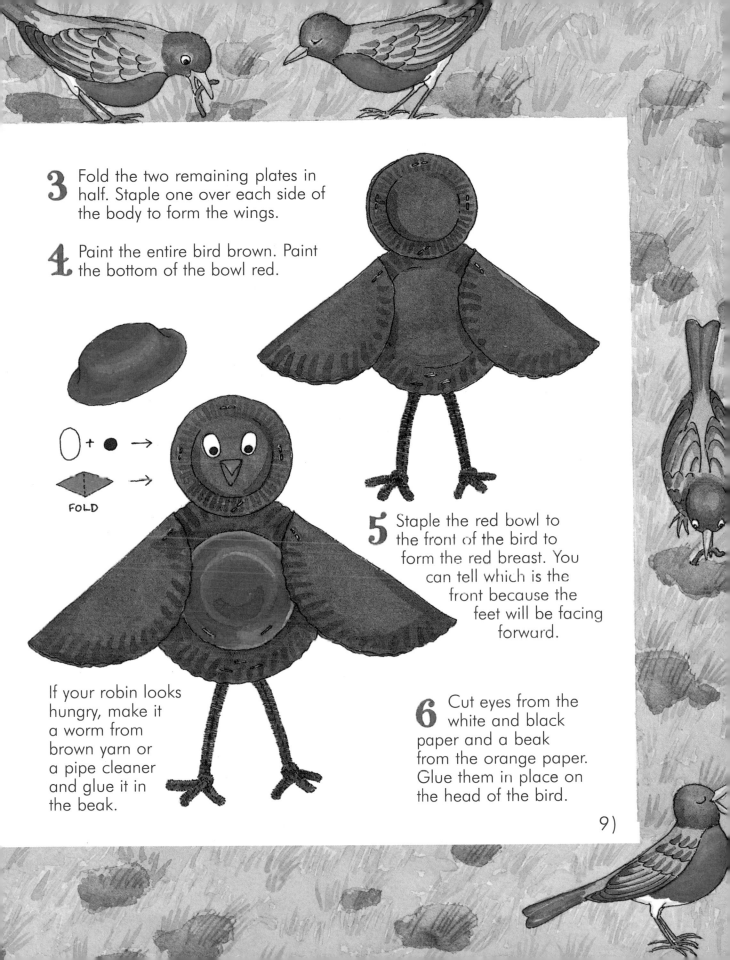

FOLD

5 Staple the red bowl to the front of the bird to form the red breast. You can tell which is the front because the feet will be facing forward.

If your robin looks hungry, make it a worm from brown yarn or a pipe cleaner and glue it in the beak.

6 Cut eyes from the white and black paper and a beak from the orange paper. Glue them in place on the head of the bird.

9)

It is said that March comes in like a lion and goes out like a lamb.

Lion and Lamb Necklace

Here is what you need:

 two pry-off bottle caps

 two cotton swabs

 one cotton ball

 three tiny wiggle eyes

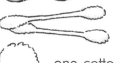 48-inch (122-cm) piece of yellow yarn

 orange and tan felt scraps

 black poster paint

 white glue

 scissors

 Styrofoam tray for drying

 masking tape

Here is what you do:

1 Dip three of the four cotton swab ends in the black paint and let them dry on the Styrofoam tray. When they are dry, cut the tips off.

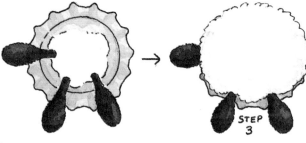

2 Fill one bottle cap with glue. Arrange one black swab sticking out off the side of the cap to form the head of the lamb. Put the other two sticking out of the bottom of the cap for the legs.

(10

3 Cover the cap with the cotton ball. If the cotton ball you are using is large, you may want to cut it so that it will fit in the cap neatly.

4 Glue a tiny wiggle eye on the head of the lamb.

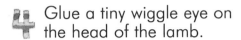

5 To make the lion, fill the second cap with glue. Cut about twenty 1-inch (2.5-cm) pieces of yellow yarn. Arrange them so that one end of each strand sticks out around the cap to make the mane of the lion.

6 Cut a circle of orange felt to glue in the cap. Cut tiny ears from the tan felt and glue them in place. Glue on two wiggle eyes.

7 Put a piece of masking tape on the back of each cap to make a better gluing surface. Cut the yellow yarn to a good necklace length for you. Glue the two caps together, back to back, with the two ends of the yarn in between to form a necklace.

When the weather is cold and windy, wear the lion side of the necklace. When it is mild and springlike, wear the lamb side.

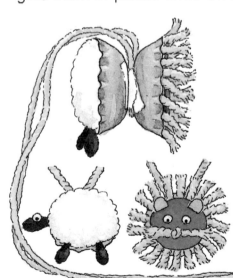

11)

The month of March is often very windy.

Huffing and Puffing Mr. Wind Puppet

Here is what you need:

 four 9-inch (23-cm) paper plates

 masking tape

 white Styrofoam cup

 light blue tissue paper

 fiberfill

 white glue

 two wiggle eyes

 scissors

 liquid detergent bottle with pull-up cap

 newspaper to work on

 stapler

Here is what you do:

1 Staple two of the plates together to make one sturdier plate. Do the same with the other two plates. Hold the two doubled plates together with the eating sides facing each other and staple them together on each side. This will be the body of the wind puppet.

2 Glue fiberfill all over both sides of the puppet.

(12

3 Cut the bottom out of the Styrofoam cup. Cut a 12-inch (30-cm) square of blue tissue paper and poke a large hole in the center of the square. Tuck the square into the open bottom of the cup so that the tissue sticks out. Tape the tissue to the inside of the cup, making sure that the hole you poked in the tissue is placed so that the cup is not blocked closed by the tissue. This will be the blowing mouth of the wind.

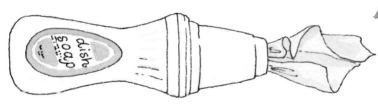

4 Pull open the top of the detergent bottle. Place the cup upside down over the top of the bottle and tape it in place. Slide the cup assembly, cup end first, between the plates of the wind body so that the tissue and the bottom edge of the cup stick out one side for the mouth. Add more staples to the top and bottom of the puppet to hold the bottle more securely, but be sure you can still slide your hand into the puppet.

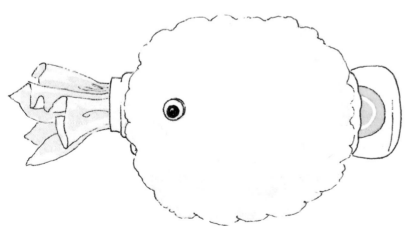

5 Glue a wiggle eye on each side of the puppet behind the mouth.

To make Mr. Wind huff and puff, just squeeze the bottle inside the puppet. You might want to cut some hats and leaves from the tissue paper for Mr. Wind to blow around.

13)

**Make this unusual wind sock
to sway in the spring breezes.**

Necktie Windsock

Here is what you need:

ten old neckties

various trims and rickracks

scissors

stapler

12- by 18-inch
(30- by 46-cm)
piece of
construction
paper

yarn

white glue

Here is what you do:

1 Cut the ten neckties in half across the center of each tie. You will be using the thinner half of each tie for this project.

10 ×

2 Fold 4 inches (10 cm) of the construction paper over lengthwise to make a strip. Trim off the extra paper along the bottom of the strip.

4"

14

3 Open the folded strip and rub glue all over the inside of the paper. Arrange the cut ends of the ten neckties facedown and side by side along the edge of the folded paper. You will not have enough ties to go to the end of the strip. Fold the top of the gluey paper over the tie ends to hold them in place.

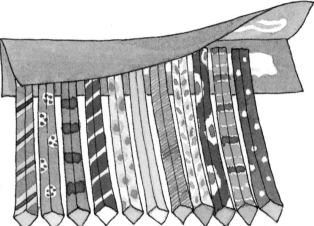

4 Carefully wrap the strip of paper around itself until you have a continuous circle of ties. Staple the strip to hold it in place. Let the glue dry.

5 Cut pieces of trim and rickrack to fit round the paper ring. Use glue to hold them in place.

6 Cut three 24-inch (61-cm) pieces of yarn to use for hangers. String the yarn pieces under the paper ring in three different places, then tie the ends together at the top.

Hang your wind sock outdoors for the wind to play with, but don't let it get wet!

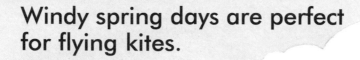

Hanger Kite Decoration

Here is what you need:

wire coat hanger

black and white construction paper

bright-colored pom-pom

three bow-shaped pieces of macaroni

white glue

old pair of brightly colored tights

red nail polish

12-inch (30-cm) pipe cleaner or sparkle stem

scissors

plastic lid for drying

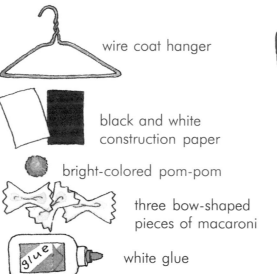

Here is what you do:

1 Bend the wire hanger into the diamond shape of a kite. Cut one leg off the tights and use it to cover the hanger, starting at the bottom of the hanger. Knot the open end of the tights behind the hook of the hanger, making sure that the tights are pulled tight. Trim the excess material off the knot.

(16

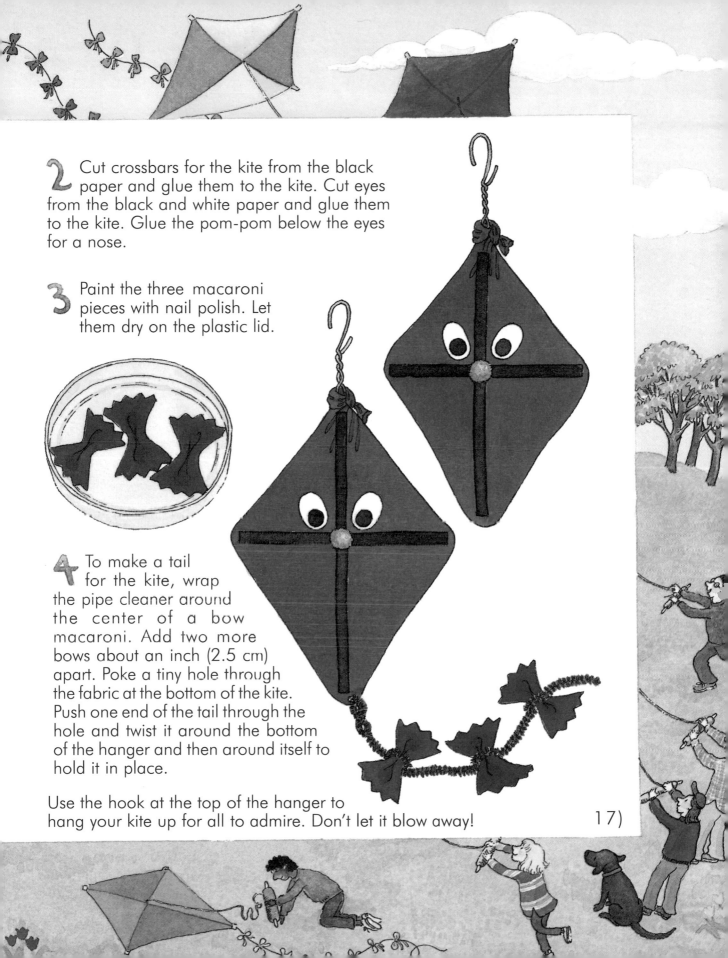

2 Cut crossbars for the kite from the black paper and glue them to the kite. Cut eyes from the black and white paper and glue them to the kite. Glue the pom-pom below the eyes for a nose.

3 Paint the three macaroni pieces with nail polish. Let them dry on the plastic lid.

4 To make a tail for the kite, wrap the pipe cleaner around the center of a bow macaroni. Add two more bows about an inch (2.5 cm) apart. Poke a tiny hole through the fabric at the bottom of the kite. Push one end of the tail through the hole and twist it around the bottom of the hanger and then around itself to hold it in place.

Use the hook at the top of the hanger to hang your kite up for all to admire. Don't let it blow away!

17)

Giant Shamrock

Here is what you need:

four 9-inch (23-cm) paper plates

hole punch

green poster paint and a paintbrush

gold glitter

white glue

scissors

yarn

paper cup and craft stick for mixing

stapler

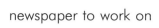
newspaper to work on

Here is what you do:

1 Cut one side of each of the paper plates to look like the top of a heart. These will be the three leaves of the shamrock. Staple them together with the bumps on the outer edge to form the shamrock.

2 Cut a curved stem from the rim of the remaining paper plate. Staple it to the bottom of the shamrock.

3 Mix one part glue to two parts green paint in the paper cup. Paint the entire shamrock quickly, then sprinkle it with glitter while the glue and paint mixture is still wet.

4 Punch a hole in the top of the shamrock. Cut a 12-inch (30-cm) piece of yarn. Thread it through the hole and tie the two ends together to make a hanger.

This shamrock is too big to be carried off by the "little people."

Do you think there is really a pot of gold at the end of the rainbow?

End-of-the-Rainbow Stabile

Here is what you need:

 one 1½-inch (1-cm) Styrofoam ball

 a small jar with an opening that the Styrofoam ball will fit through

 fiberfill

 scissors

 white glue

 12-inch (30-cm) pipe cleaners, one each in red, orange, yellow, green, blue, and purple

old black sock

 gold glitter

 masking tape

Here is what you do:

1 Ask an adult to cut the Styrofoam ball in half. Hold one of the halves flat side down and stick the end of each of the pipe cleaners into the top of the ball, side by side, left to right, in the order shown in the picture.

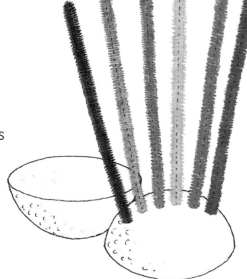

2 Lay the pipe cleaners down flat on a counter with the ball just over the edge of the counter. Tape the pipe cleaners to the counter just above the Styrofoam ball. Curve the pipe cleaners around to form a rainbow, and tape the other ends to the counter. Trim the ends so they are even. Push the ends into the top of the other half of the Styrofoam ball.

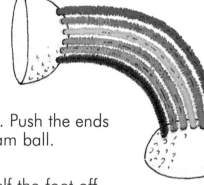

3 Cut about half the foot off the black sock. Put the jar into the toe of the sock. Fold the ends down into the jar.

4 Remove the tape and pick up the rainbow. Stick one of the Styrofoam ball ends into the jar. Cover it with glue, then fill the remainder of the jar with fiberfill. Cover the fiberfill with glue and sprinkle it with gold glitter.

5 Rub glue over the Styrofoam ball half at the other end of the rainbow. Cover the ball with fiberfill so it looks like a cloud.

This rainbow will stay around in any kind of weather.

In the spring, many animals wake up from a long winter nap.

Wake-up Bear Bag Puppet

Here is what you need:

 brown lunch bag

 black, brown, and white construction paper

 white glue

scissors

markers

 pencil

Here is what you do:

1 Turn the bag upside down so that the bottom of the bag becomes the top of the bear puppet. Cut two eyes from white paper small enough to be hidden under the fold that was the bottom of the bag. Cut pupils from black paper to glue on each eye. Glue the eyes under the fold of the bag so they are hidden.

2 Cut two strips of black paper and fringe the edges to make eyelashes. Curl the paper lashes around a pencil to make them tip out slightly. Glue them to the bag bottom (that is now the head of the bear) over each eye.

3 Cut ears, nose, and arms from the brown construction paper and glue them in place. Cut two nostrils from black paper to glue on the nose.

4 Use a marker to add to the bear any details you wish.

To wake up your sleeping bear, just slip your hand inside the bag and lift up the flap. Happy springtime, Bear!

23)

Crocuses are one of the first flowers to appear in the spring.

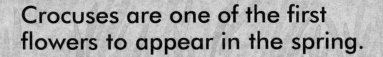
Crocus Dish Garden

Here is what you need:

 small margarine tub with lid

 one 1½-inch (1-cm) Styrofoam ball

 Easter grass

 scissors

 white glue

 one yellow and three green 12-inch (30-cm) pipe cleaners

 blue plastic wrap

 green plastic tape

 3 plastic spoons

 pink or purple nail polish

 masking tape

 ribbon

Here is what you do:

1 Paint both sides of the bowls of the three spoons with nail polish. Place them to dry on the plastic lid from the margarine tub.

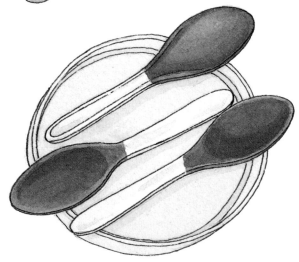

2 Cover the bottom of the inside of the margarine tub with masking tape. Cut the Styrofoam ball in half and cover the flat side of one half with a strip of masking tape. (Put the other half aside for another project). Glue the ball, taped side down, in the center of the margarine tub.

3 Fold the yellow pipe cleaner in half. Hold the three spoons, with the bowls curving in, around the folded pipe cleaner to look like petals around the stamen of the flower. Wrap green tape around the handles of the spoons to hold them in place and to make the stem of the flower.

4 Press the bottom of the flower into the center of the Styrofoam ball in the margarine tub. Fold each of the three green pipe cleaners in half and stick the ends in the Styrofoam around the base of the flower to make leaves.

5 Rub glue all over the Styrofoam around the flower and cover it with Easter grass. Use ribbon to tie a square of blue plastic wrap around the margarine tub.

You can enjoy this pretty symbol of spring any time of the year.

25)

Many people find the sound of spring rain very soothing.

Pitter-patter Rain Stick

Here is what you need:

 long cardboard tube from gift wrap

 uncooked rice

aluminum foil

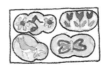 spring stickers

Here is what you do:

1 Tear off a strip of aluminum foil about one and a half times as long as the cardboard tube. Squeeze the sides of the foil together to make a long snakelike strip.

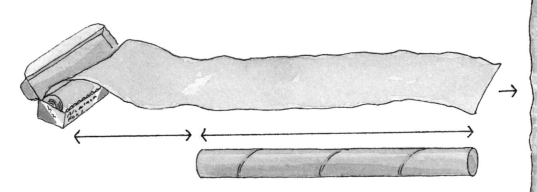

2 Tear off a second strip of foil that is 6 inches (15 cm) longer than the cardboard tube. Wrap the foil around the tube so that there are about 3 extra inches (8 cm) sticking out from each end of the tube. Fold the extra foil over at one end of the tube to close that end.

3 Bend the long strip of foil into a zigzag shape so that it will fit inside the tube. Slide it in. Drop in a handful of rice. Seal the open end of the tube by folding over the extra foil. Be sure you haven't left anyplace where the rice could fall out!

4 Decorate the rain stick with pretty spring stickers.

To hear the pleasing sound of falling rain just tip the stick, hold it still, and listen.

In many places, springtime means the arrival of lots of pretty birds.

Spring Bird Mask

Here is what you need:

 two 9-inch (23-cm) paper plates

 cardboard paper towel tube

 poster paints and a paintbrush

newspaper to work on

 two white or light-colored oval-shaped shoulder pads

 craft feathers

white glue

scissors

Styrofoam tray for drying

Here is what you do:

1 Glue the two plates together to make them stronger. Cut two eyeholes from the plate. Paint the bottom of the plate in the color of your choice. You can make your mask to look like a real bird or design a colorful bird of your own.

2 Paint both sides of both shoulder pads to make the beak. Let them dry on the Styrofoam tray.

3 Cut a 2½-inch (6-cm) slit in the plate below the eyes. Stack the two shoulder pads, one on top of the other, and pull the pointed ends of one side through the slit so that the pads stick out to form the beak of the bird.

3 Glue craft feathers above the eyes of the bird to make a crest.

4 Paint the cardboard tube a bright color. Cut a 2-inch (5-cm) slit on each side of one end of the tube. Slide the bottom of the bird head into the slits so you have a holder for the bird mask.

Make masks for your friends, and you could have a whole flock of colorful birds this spring!

29)

**Springtime brings new life
to the earth.**

Spaghetti Bird's Nest

Here is what you need:

spaghetti

white glue

small margarine tub
with a lid

craft feathers

craft stick for mixing

light-blue tissue
paper

brown poster
paint

aluminum foil

Here is what you do:

1 Break enough spaghetti into small
pieces to make about a cupful.

2 Pour about ¼ cup (60 milliliters)
of glue into the margarine tub.
Color the glue with a small amount
of brown paint. Add the broken
spaghetti to the brown glue. Mix until
the spaghetti is completely brown. If
the mixture seems too dry, add a tiny
bit more glue. If it seems too wet, add
some more spaghetti pieces.

3 Press the gluey mixture around the sides and over the bottom of the margarine tub to form a nest. Let the glue dry completely before trying to remove the nest from the margarine tub.

4 Shape three small eggs for the nest from aluminum foil. Rub each egg with glue and wrap it in light-blue tissue paper. Let the eggs dry on the plastic lid from the margarine tub.

Line the nest with two or three colorful craft feathers before placing the eggs in the nest.

31)

The Jewish holiday of Passover is celebrated in the spring.

Passover Candlesticks

Here is what you need:

 two small jars

 two candles

old costume jewelry

 aluminum foil

ribbon

Here is what you do:

1 For each candleholder, tear off a square of aluminum foil. Press the center of the foil square down into the jar and mold the foil to the inside shape of the jar.

2 Slip pretty jewels into the jar between the foil and the side of the jar. Earrings are nice for this project because you can use one of each pair in each candleholder to make them match.

"WHY IS THIS NIGHT DIFFERENT FROM ALL OTHER NIGHTS?"

3 Wrap a small ball of foil around the base of one of the candles. Set the candle in the center of the jar and pack foil tightly around it until the jar is full and the candle is standing.

4 Tie a piece of pretty ribbon around the neck of the candleholder.

It is best to remove the ribbon before you light the candle.

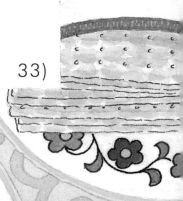

33)

The Christian celebration of Easter takes place in the spring.

Easter Bunny Egg Holder

Here is what you need:

white Styrofoam cup

pink ribbon

ballpoint pen

pink marker

scissors

Here is what you do:

1 Draw a line around the cup that is 1inch (2.5 cm) above the bottom. On one side draw the head and ears of a bunny with the bottom of the head touching the line around the cup.

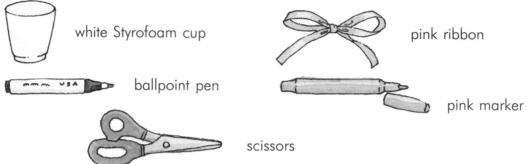

2 Cut away all of the cup around the head of the bunny and above the line around the front and sides of the cup.

(34

3 Use the pen to draw a face on the bunny on the inside part of the cup. Color the inner ears and nose with the pink marker.

4 Draw paws on the outside front of the base of the cup so that it will look like the bunny has its arms around a great big egg.

5 Tie a ribbon around the neck of the bunny.

This bunny is perfect for displaying your prettiest Easter egg.

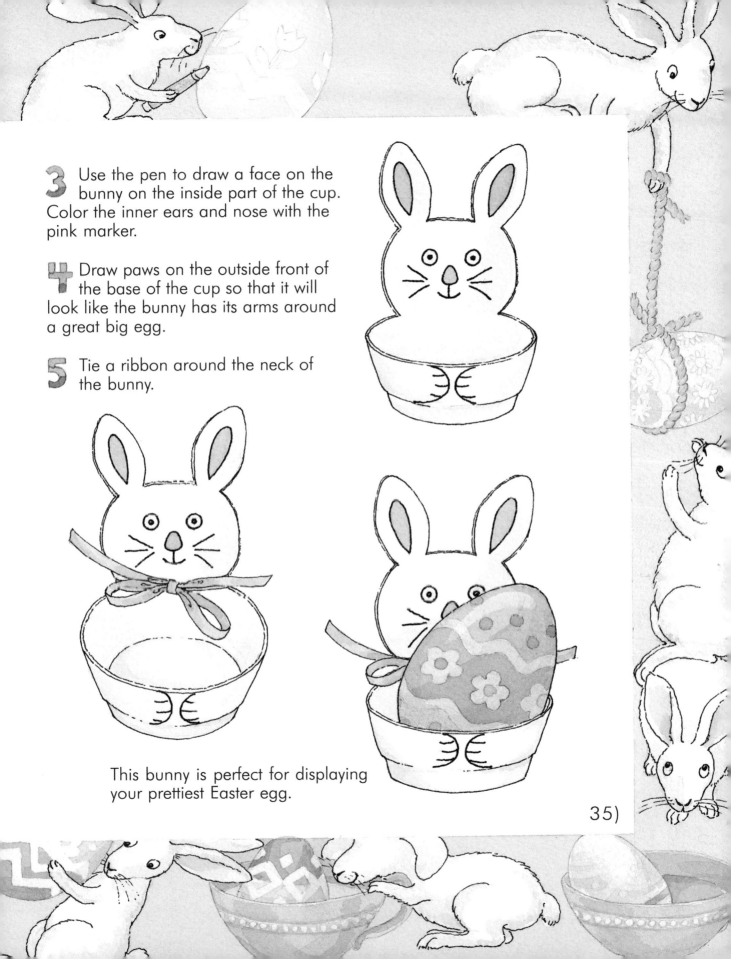

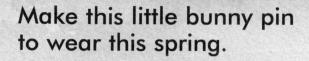

Wooden Spoons Bunny Pin

Here is what you need:

 two wooden ice-cream spoons

 margarine tub

 masking tape

 white glue

 Styrofoam tray to work on

 white poster paint and a paintbrush

 clear glitter

 two wiggle eyes

 small pink pom-pom

 safety pin

 thin pink ribbon

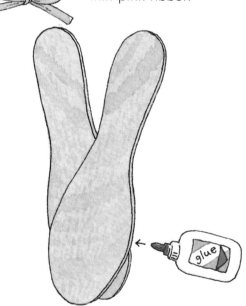

Here is what you do:

1 Glue the spoon end of the two sticks together at an angle so that the two handles form a V shape for the bunny's ears and the front spoon end forms the head.

(36

2 Mix one part glue with two parts white paint in the margarine tub. Paint the bunny white, then quickly sprinkle over the paint with clear glitter.

3 Glue two wiggle eyes and a pom-pom nose on the head of the bunny. Tie a piece of pink ribbon in a bow. Glue the bow just below the ears of the bunny.

4 Glue the safety pin to the back of the bunny. Use masking tape to hold the pin in place while the glue dries.

This bunny pin would make a nice gift for your mom or a friend. Maybe you should make more than one.

Make this little white duck using the shape of your own hands and foot.

Little White Duck

Here is what you need:

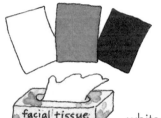 white, black, and orange construction paper

 white facial tissue

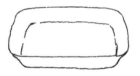 white glue

 pencil

 scissors

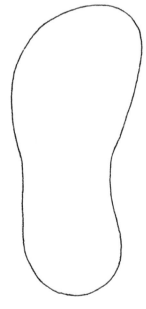 Styrofoam tray for drying

Here is what you do:

1 Trace around your two hands on the white paper and cut them out. Trace around one of your feet on the white paper and cut it out.

2 Turn the foot shape so that the heel of your foot will form the head of the duck. Glue a hand shape on each side of the foot, below the heel, to form the wings of the duck.

3 Shred some white facial tissue and glue it all over the duck for feathers.

4 Cut a bill for the duck by folding a piece of orange paper and cutting a bill shape. Glue the back of the bill on the face of the duck. Glue on two eyes cut from black paper. Cut two webbed feet from the orange paper. Glue the top of each foot behind the bottom of the duck so that they hang down from the bottom.

Warning! Better keep this little white duck away from the water!

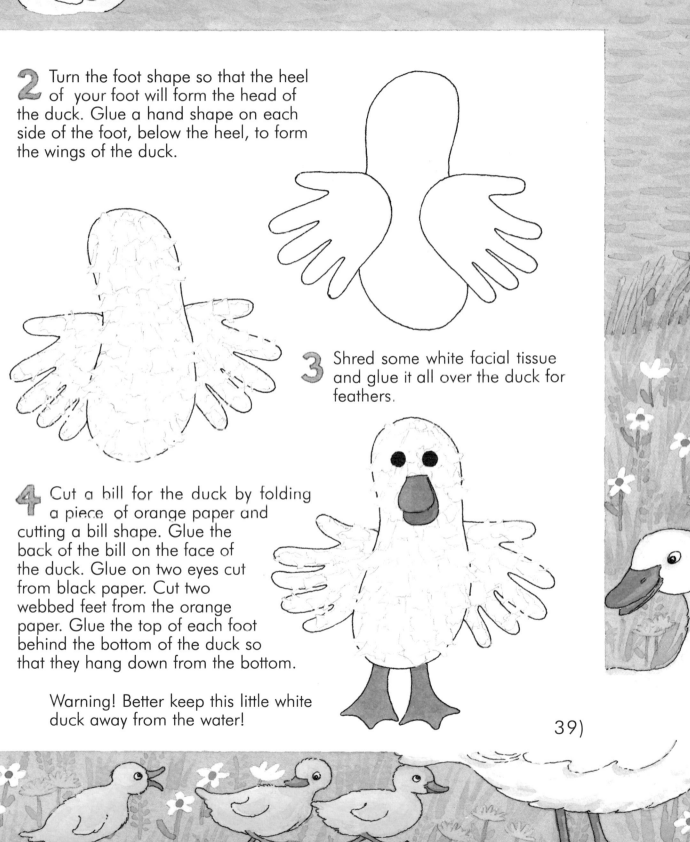

39)

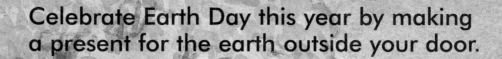

Celebrate Earth Day this year by making a present for the earth outside your door.

Flower Sprinkle Bottle

Here is what you need:

2-quart (2-liter) plastic soda bottle with cap

nail polish

plastic tape in two or more colors

scissors

nail

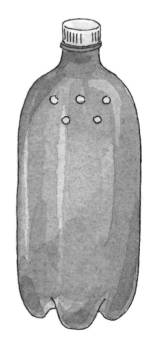

Here is what you do:

1. Ask an adult to use a nail to poke five or more holes in the top side of the bottle.

2 Paint the bottle cap with nail polish.

3 Decorate the bottle using pieces of the colored tape.

Fill your sprinkle bottle with water, then put the cap back on. Now, go outside and give the flowers a gentle drink.

41)

Growing Flower

Here is what you need:

old tube of lipstick

 stapler

6-inch (15-cm) red and 6-inch green pipe cleaner

scissors

brown construction paper

craft stick

Here is what you do:

1 Turn the lipstick all the way up in the tube. Use the craft stick to scrape the lipstick off level with the inner case.

2 Cut a 4-inch (10-cm) piece of green pipe cleaner for the flower stem. Wrap the remaining piece around the upper part of the stem to make leaves. Shape a flower from the red pipe cleaner. Attach it to the top of the stem.

(42

3 Push the bottom of the flower stem down into the remaining lipstick in the tube.

4 Cut the front and the back of a flowerpot from the brown paper. Make the pot as tall as the lipstick tube. Staple the two sides of the front and the back of the pot together with the tube between them.

To make the flower grow, just turn the outer case of the lipstick tube. This flower grows without the rain!

TURN LIPSTICK TUBE HERE

Get ready to help with the "spring cleaning."

Spring Cleaning Apron

Here is what you need:

roll of white paper towels

ribbon

stapler

marker

Here is what you do:

1 Tear off a strip of three paper towels, leaving them attached. Make a flat pile of six strips of three paper towels each.

2 Cut a piece of ribbon long enough for the person using the apron to tie around his or her waist.

Spring Cleaning Apron
Tear off paper towels as needed

3 Fold the pile of towels in half over the center of the ribbon to make an apron. Staple the towels together on each side to hold them in place.

4 Use the marker to write "Spring Cleaning Apron" and "Tear off paper towels as needed."

This handy apron will keep the wearer supplied with paper towels for a whole day of spring cleaning.

45)

Make your own little lamb to play with this spring.

Fluffy Toy Lamb

Here is what you need:

black knit glove

 fiberfill

2 wiggle eyes

 thin ribbon

scissors

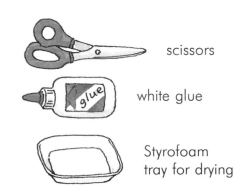 white glue

Styrofoam
tray for drying

Here is what you do:

1 Stuff the glove with fiberfill. Tuck the open end of the glove down into itself to close it. This will be the body of the lamb. The thumb of the glove will be the head of the lamb, and the fingers will be the legs.

(46

2 Rub glue all over the front and back of the hand portion of the glove. Wrap the glove in fiberfill to give the lamb a fluffy coat.

3 Tie a bow around the base of the thumb of the glove.

4 Glue a wiggle eye on each side of the thumb.

BAA! Who said that?

47)

In some places, children dance around the "Maypole" to celebrate the first day of May.

Maypole Hat

Here is what you need:

 cardboard paper-towel tube

 pencil

 paper bowl

 ribbon in several different colors

 white glue

 newspaper to work on

hole punch

scissors

green poster paint and a paintbrush

artificial flowers

Here is what you do:

1 Trace around the end of the paper-towel tube on the center of the bottom of the bowl. Cut the traced circle out of the bowl.

2 Cut several 1-inch (2.5-cm)-deep slits around one end of the tube. Slip the cut end of the tube into the hole on the bottom of the bowl. Spread the slits out and glue them to the inside of the bowl to hold the tube in place. This will be the Maypole.

(48

3 Paint the Maypole green and let it dry.

4 Cut eight or more 18-inch (46-cm) pieces of ribbon. Rub glue around the inside of the top of the tube. Press the ends of each ribbon down into the glue in the top of the tube. Arrange the ribbons so that they hang down around the tube pole. Dip the ends of some artificial flowers in glue and tuck them in the top of the pole.

5 Punch a hole on each side of the bowl. Tie the end of a 24-inch (61-cm) piece of ribbon through each hole so that the Maypole can be tied on to wear as a hat.

Put on the hat, twirl around, and pretend you are a Maypole!

Springtime means lots of creeping, crawling things!

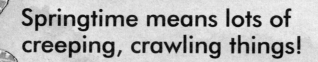

Sock Caterpillar

Here is what you need:

 scissors

 child-size white sock

 two wiggle eyes

 old socks for stuffing

 white glue

cardboard paper-towel or toilet-tissue tube

 6-inch (15-cm) green pipe cleaner or sparkle stem

 green and yellow poster paint and a paintbrush

 Styrofoam tray for drying

Here is what you do:

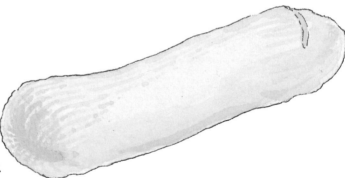

1 Stuff the small sock to make a caterpillar body. Tuck the open end of the sock down into itself on one side to close the sock and form a mouth for the caterpillar.

2 Paint the entire caterpillar body yellow.

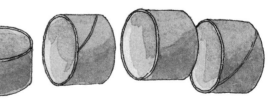

3 Cut four 1-inch (2.5-cm)-wide rings from the cardboard tube. Paint the rings green.

4 Slide the rings over the body of the caterpillar and arrange them so they are evenly spaced to give the caterpillar stripes. Glue the rings in place.

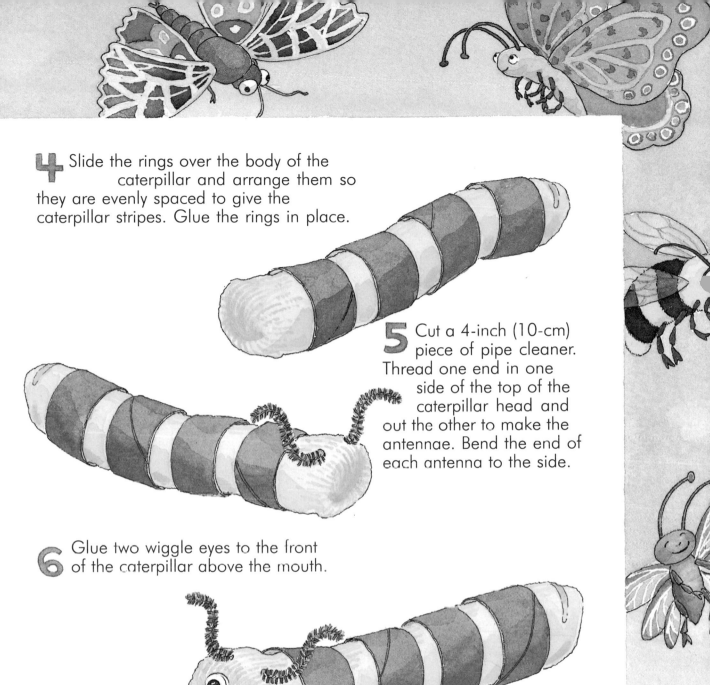

5 Cut a 4-inch (10-cm) piece of pipe cleaner. Thread one end in one side of the top of the caterpillar head and out the other to make the antennae. Bend the end of each antenna to the side.

6 Glue two wiggle eyes to the front of the caterpillar above the mouth.

You might want to make your creepy, crawly caterpillar in a different combination of colors.

Design your own butterfly with this project.

Plastic Bag Butterfly

Here is what you need:

 wooden clamp clothespin

 6-inch (15-cm) pipe cleaner

 2 wiggle eyes

 yellow poster paint and a paintbrush

 white glue

 gallon-size plastic bag

 stapler

 colorful pieces of tissue paper

mylar from deflated balloons

 confetti

 sticky-back magnet

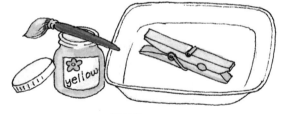 Styrofoam tray for drying

Here is what you do:

1 Paint the clothespin yellow and let it dry.

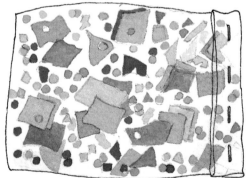

2 Fill the plastic bag lightly with colorful bits of tissue paper, confetti, and mylar. Fold the open end of the bag over and staple along the fold to hold it shut.

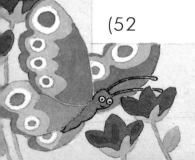

3 Gather the bag together at the center, and slide it in between the clamps of the clothespin.

4 Shape the ends of the pipe cleaner into antennae. Glue the center of the pipe cleaner between the clamps of the clothespin.

5 Press a piece of sticky-back magnet on the back of the butterfly.

Surprise someone you know by sticking a beautiful spring butterfly to their refrigerator!

53)

Make a vase to hold some sweet-smelling spring flowers.

Vase for Spring Flowers

Here is what you need:

 16-ounce (454-gram) can, empty, with the top cut off

 9-ounce (255-gram) plastic cup to fit exactly inside the can

 colorful woman's sock

 masking tape

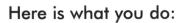 ribbons and trims

 felt in a color that looks nice with the sock

 white glue

 scissors

 ballpoint pen

Here is what you do:

1 Cut the foot off the sock. Use the cuff of the sock to cover the can. Push the cup down into the can to hold the sock in place at the top.

2 Use masking tape to tape the bottom of the sock flat against the bottom of the can.

(54

3 Trace around the bottom of the can on the felt. Cut the felt circle out and glue it over the taped bottom of the can.

4 Use lace, ribbon, or other trims to decorate the sock-covered can.

You might want to make the "bottle bottom flowers" on page 56 to put in your vase when real flowers aren't available.

Bottle Bottom Flowers

Here is what you need:

 16-ounce (454-milliliter) plastic soda bottle

 yellow and green construction paper

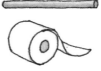 green plastic straw

 scissors

 clear packing tape

 colored glue

 hole punch

Here is what you do:

1 Have an adult help you cut the bottom off of the plastic soda bottle about 1 inch (2.5 cm) up from the bottom. This will give you a very nice flower shape.

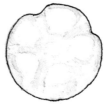

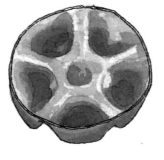

2 Color the plastic flower by covering the inside of the bottle bottom with colored glue. Let the glue dry completely before continuing. This could take up to two days.

3 Cut a yellow construction paper center for the flower. Use a piece of rolled packing tape to attach the center to the flower.

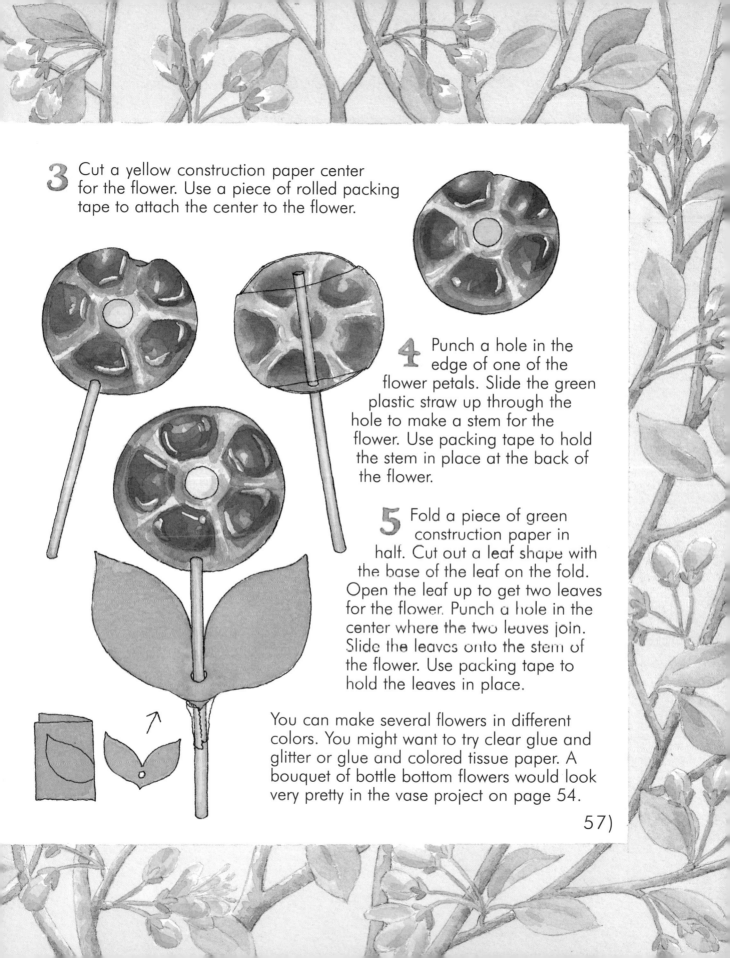

4 Punch a hole in the edge of one of the flower petals. Slide the green plastic straw up through the hole to make a stem for the flower. Use packing tape to hold the stem in place at the back of the flower.

5 Fold a piece of green construction paper in half. Cut out a leaf shape with the base of the leaf on the fold. Open the leaf up to get two leaves for the flower. Punch a hole in the center where the two leaves join. Slide the leaves onto the stem of the flower. Use packing tape to hold the leaves in place.

You can make several flowers in different colors. You might want to try clear glue and glitter or glue and colored tissue paper. A bouquet of bottle bottom flowers would look very pretty in the vase project on page 54.

57)

Design your own bugs this spring.

Pocket Puppet Bugs

Here is what you need:

old shirt with a pocket

four 12-inch (30-cm) pipe cleaners

two black pom-poms or wiggle eye

scissors

white glue

Here is what you do:

1 Cut around the pocket of an old shirt to remove it. The pocket will be the body of the bug puppet.

2 Cut a small slit in the middle of the seam on each side of the pocket. Slide pipe cleaners in one slit, across the pocket and out the other side, so that the same amount of pipe cleaner sticks out on each side of the pocket. Bend the pipe cleaners to make legs for the bug.

3 Cut two small slits on one side of the pocket, toward the bottom seam. Cut a 6-inch (15-cm) piece of pipe cleaner. Slide the pipe cleaner in one slit and out the other. Shape the two ends of the pipe cleaner into antennae for the bug.

4 Glue two pom-poms or wiggle eyes just above the bottom of the pocket.

To use your bug puppet, just slip your hand into the pocket and walk it around. You might want to add wings cut from a dryer sheet or button spots. What other ideas can you think of for your bug?

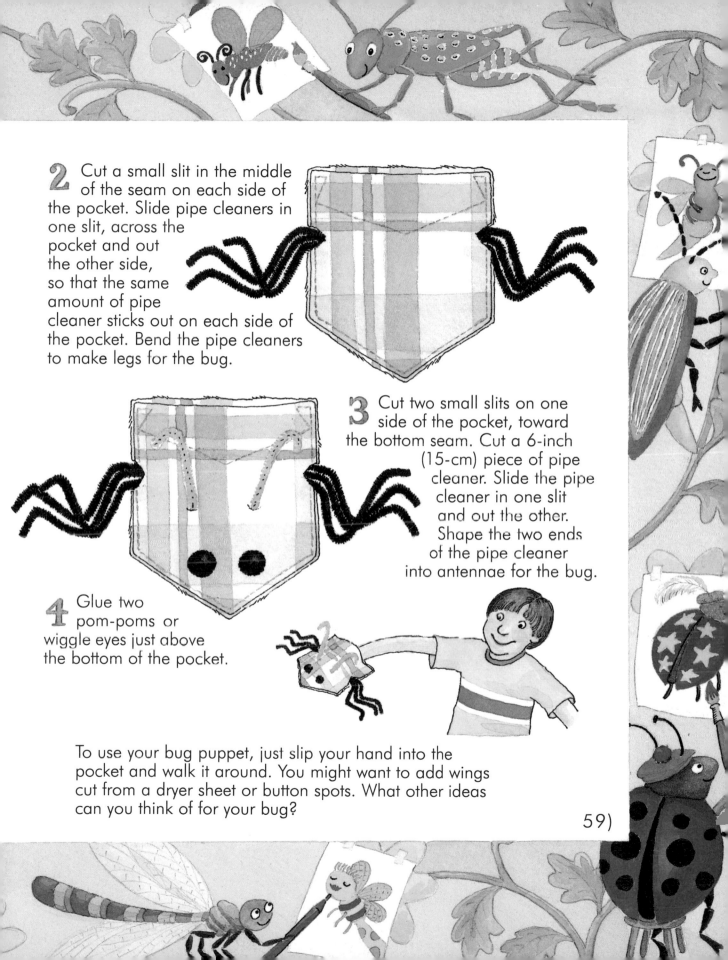

In the springtime, tadpoles hatch and change into frogs.

Tadpole to Frog Puppet

Here is what you need:

 two teardrop-shaped shoulder pads, green if possible

 green, blue, yellow, and brown felt

white glue

scissors

 hole punch

blue yarn

Here is what you do:

1 Hold the two shoulder pads together with the raised sides facing out. Punch a hole in the center of each side of each shoulder pad. Cut two 5-inch (13-cm) pieces of yarn. Use the yarn to tie the shoulder pads together through the holes on each side. You should now be able to easily turn the shoulder pads inside out and back again.

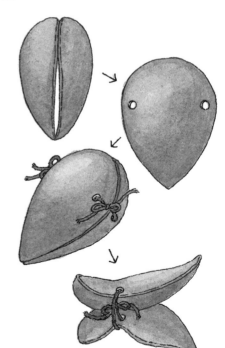

2 Leave the shoulder pads turned inside out with the raised sides facing in. Cut back and front frog legs from green felt. Glue the back

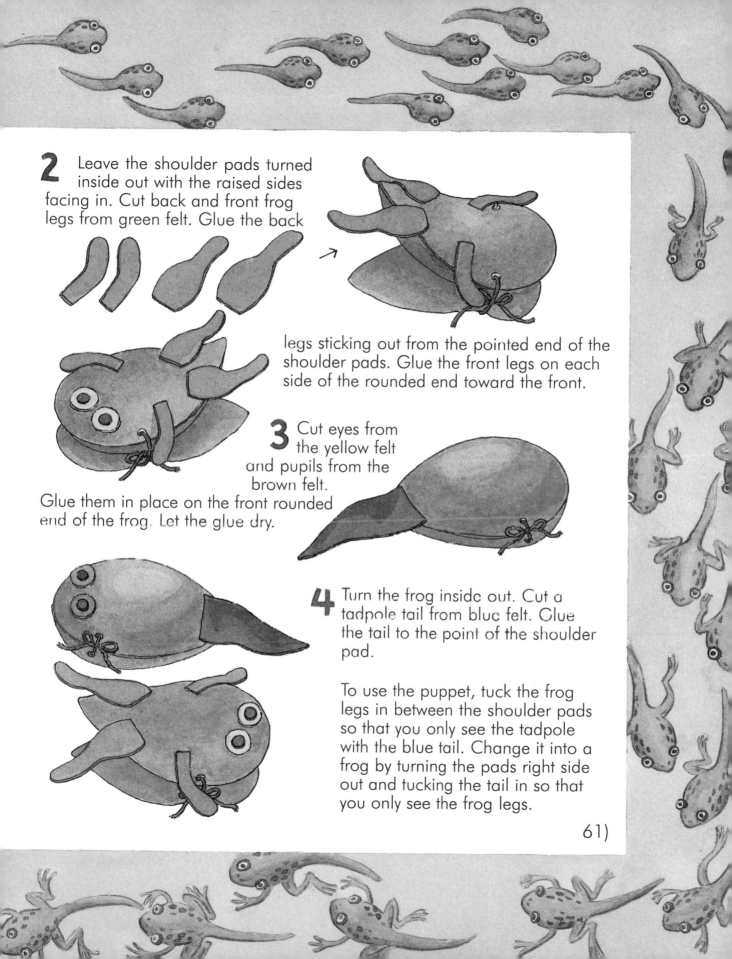

legs sticking out from the pointed end of the shoulder pads. Glue the front legs on each side of the rounded end toward the front.

3 Cut eyes from the yellow felt and pupils from the brown felt. Glue them in place on the front rounded end of the frog. Let the glue dry.

4 Turn the frog inside out. Cut a tadpole tail from blue felt. Glue the tail to the point of the shoulder pad.

To use the puppet, tuck the frog legs in between the shoulder pads so that you only see the tadpole with the blue tail. Change it into a frog by turning the pads right side out and tucking the tail in so that you only see the frog legs.

61)

Make this pretty photo album for your mom or grandmother on Mother's Day.

Box Photo Album

Here is what you need:

five square facial tissue boxes

pretty ribbon

white glue

scissors

about twenty paper clips

hole punch

pencil

Here is what you do:

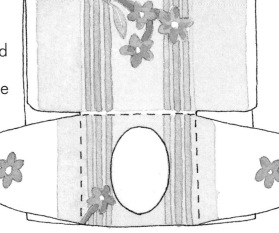

1. Carefully pull apart the glued seams of each box so that it lies flat. Fold the top of one of the boxes over onto one of the sides so that the pattern is around the oval and the pattern is on the side facing out.

2. Cut around the square top and side of the box to form a small picture frame. Glue the two sides of the frame shut, but leave the top open to slide a picture in. Use paper clips to hold the cardboard together while the glue dries. Make at least five picture frame pages for the album.

3 To make the front and back cover for the album, cut four squares from remaining sides of the box. They should be the same size as your frame pages. Glue two squares together, print side out, for the front of the book. Do the same with the other two squares to make the back cover of the book. Use paper clips to hold the cardboard together while the glue dries.

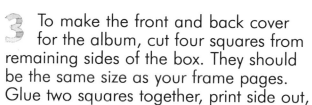

4 Stack the covers and album pages together in the order you want them to be. Punch two holes in the left side of the cover page. Use a pencil to mark where to punch the holes in the next page. Keep doing this until all the pages have holes.

5 Use ribbon to tic two pages together. Tie the ribbon in a bow on the front side of the album.

Make this gift extra special by slipping a picture of you into the frame on the first page.

63)

About the Author and Artist

Twenty years as a teacher and director of nursery-school programs in Oneida, New York, have given Kathy Ross extensive experience in guiding children through craft projects. A collector of teddy bears and paper dolls, she frequently has had her craft projects published in *Highlights* magazine. She is the author of Millbrook's Holiday Crafts for Kids series and Crafts for Kids Who Are Wild About series. She is also the author of *Gifts to Make for Your Favorite Grown-ups, The Best Holiday Craft Book Ever, Crafts From Your Favorite Fairy Tales,* and *The Jewish Holiday Craft Book.*

A resident of Andover, Massachusetts, Vicky Enright majored in editorial design/illustration at Syracuse University. To date, she has utilized her talents as a calligrapher, a wallpaper designer, and a greeting-card illustrator. Her first book was *Crafts From Your Favorite Fairy Tales* by Kathy Ross.